AF335158

LOVE and WAR

(A Treatise and World World II Memoir)

by

Robert W. "Bob" Buntin

Alexander Books

Alexander, North Carolina

This book is dedicated to man's work for the absence of war and his search for that inner peace which passeth all understanding.

– Bob Buntin

Publisher: Ralph Roberts

Cover Design: Ralph Roberts

Editor: Ralph Roberts, Pat Roberts

Interior Design and Electronic Page Assembly: **WorldComm**®

Printed in the United States of America

10 9 8 7 6 5 4 3 2 1

ISBN 978-1-57090-261-1 Trade Paper

ISBN 978-1-57090-262-8 Casebound

Alexander Books—a publishing imprint of Creativity, Inc.–is a full-service publisher located at 65 Macedonia Road, Alexander NC 28701. Phone (828) 252-9515 or (828) 255-8719 fax. For orders only: 1-800-472-0438. Visa and MasterCard accepted.

Alexander Books is distributed to the trade by **aBOOKS** 65 Macedonia Road, Alexander NC 28701. To order, call 1-800-472-0438.

This book is also available on the Internet along with our other books. Set your browser to **http://abooks.com** and enjoy the many fine values available.

CONTENTS

Bob Buntin at different times in his life. Small inset in upper left, revisiting Zwickau, Germany in 1999. Large photo in center, Bob at age 16. Inset lower right, Bob Buntin, August 1945, age 20 at Fort Sill, Oklahoma.

Preface

I would like and prefer this to be an autobiography, but I see no sense if I cannot tell the truth, the whole truth, and nothing but the truth. I would be too ashamed and not have the courage to be that honest. Therefore, I fear the reader will find only some sort of philosophical muddling about our country's state of affairs and life's meaning.

Prior to their holding the highest office in the land, two of our presidents were postmasters. President John F. Kennedy, a Democrat, appointed me postmaster of Blackstone, Virginia in 1963, just over a month before his assassination.

President Andrew Jackson, a Democrat, appointed Abraham Lincoln, a Republican, postmaster in 1833. What could have possessed Jackson to do such a thing? The reason is unknown but there must have been any number of qualified Democrats he could have appointed to be postmaster of New Salem, Illinois. Lincoln proved to be a good postmaster; in one instance, he was reported to have delivered the U.S. Mail, carrying some in the lining of his hat.

World War I President, Woodrow Wilson, appointed Harry Truman postmaster of Grandview, Missouri in 1914. The generous Truman refused the pay, which was about $59 per month, and directed that his pay go to a WW I postal clerk who had been widowed by the war. Postmaster appointments, like judges, were positions requiring confirmation by the U.S. Senate.

We now have a billion Islamic people mad as hell with us, who will do anything and everything they can to kill Americans. We have so many hating us because we chose the wrong course of action following the massacre of our own on September 11, 2001 by a group of suicidal murderers. Why wouldn't we want revenge, and be as certain as possible that it doesn't happen again?

It is natural to have that feeling, but our invasion of Iraq was exactly the wrong way to react. We are there now and must make the best of it until we can muster an orderly withdrawal; but withdraw we must. The same with Afghanistan, as we have been there nine years and counting, and guess what? Not much in our national interest! Thirty thousand more troops can't make a difference. Let's declare success and get the hell out. Our troops will love you for that, Mr. President.

It's bad enough having a billion people wishing us ill.

Of more concern is having our armed forces spread too thin. God forbid that we are faced with another crisis, for we are stretched to the limit. How did we get ourselves in such a predicament in the first place? That's not the right question, but it has to do with arrogance and our change in foreign policy. We are looking abroad for monsters to destroy, a preemptive solution, to get them before they get us. That has never before been an objective of our foreign policy. What we seek is peace and the absence of war, but then why do we choose war so often? It is because man loves war, contrary to his declaration otherwise. That is the debate undertaken here, the how and the why love and war are so intertwined.

Wars are the deaths of republics, but don't we know that? President Madison warned, "No nation can preserve its freedom in the midst of continual warfare." We are in great need of a long interim of peace, that we may save ourselves, our country. In *The Conscience of a Conservative*, Barry Goldwater writes, "Is it so hard when we think of the risks that were taken to create our country? – Risks on which our ancestors openly and proudly staked their lives, their fortunes, and sacred honor." Will we do any less today to save our country with the avoidance of war, staking our lives, our fortunes and sacred honor?

The phrase, *this too shall pass* is an old proverb which basically means that all things go to history in their own time; and something will take its place that will also pass on to history. *This too shall pass away* is universal wisdom, but also a warning to hold fast to our republic, and pass on our hard earned freedoms. This is not possible with our state of continual warfare.

Upon victory in Europe (VE Day), May 8, 1945, we boarded a hospital ship at Le Havre, France headed for the good ole USA. I wished to be in New York celebrating in Times Square but was happy to be quietly celebrating aboard ship headed that way. Then it hit me! What if, lurking out in the Atlantic was a German U-boat whose captain had not gotten the word the war was over? We could be torpedoed, and having survived all the shells and near starvation in a German prison only to now per-ish at sea sailing for home. The old anxiety returned as I sought reassurance from any sailor I could grab, and who appeared dumbfounded at my question about such a pos-sibility. I asked more than one to pass my concern on to his captain, requesting that he be alert for such a reality. There is always someone who doesn't get the word!

Chapter I

Christmas Eve 1944 at 9:15 in the morning the troopship SS *Leopoldville* departed Southampton, England for Cherbourg, France, ninety-five miles away across the English Channel. Lurking there in the Channel was the German U-boat *486* commanded by First Lieutenant Gerhard Meyer. This was a new German submarine built and launched in mid-February 1944 from the shipyards at Kiel, Germany. The troopship was only five miles from the entrance to Cherbourg harbor when disaster struck. *U-486* slicing through the waters with periscope up was stalking the approaching *Leopoldville* and upon command of Lieutenant Gerhard Meyer fired a salvo of torpedoes.

Aboard the ship were over 2000 soldiers of the 66th (Panther) Infantry Division being sent as reinforcements for the Battle of the Bulge, which began on 16th of December. In this small convoy was the SS *Cheshire* holding another 2000 members of the 66th Division. On this troopship was a friend of mine, Wayland H.

"Turtle" Jones, an infantry officer. Turtle had taught me in high school and was now on his way to rescue me. Of course, he did not know I was one of many in trouble, fighting in the Bulge. He would never have the chance at rescue, such was the heavy loss of life aboard the *Leopoldville* from his division.

The division was diverted to another assignment as 876 soldiers of the 66th Infantry Division perished with the sinking of the *Leopoldville*. This disaster was immediately classified top-secret and remained classified until the end of the war, and for many years thereafter. The families of the victims never knew in most instances what happened or how their loved ones died. Over 400 bodies were never recovered from the freezing waters of the Atlantic. All surviving officers and men of the division were sworn to secrecy. The enemy must not learn the magnitude of our loss.

There are dozens of stories about survivors and those attempting to survive, and the heroic efforts of officers and others trying to save their men. The British destroyer HMS *Brilliant* pulled alongside the sinking *Leopoldville* and threw a line to the doomed ship. An officer on the *Brilliant* called out, "Jump, lads, Jump! Ye may never have another chance like this!"

The two ships heaving up and down in the heavy seas made it scary and difficult to jump to the deck of the destroyer. One had to time his jump just right to make a safe landing as the gap grew and closed between the two rolling ships. One would get crushed or fall into the sea between the two ships if the timing of the jump was missed. However, most of those making a go of it landed successfully on the deck of the destroyer. These stories make one cringe and cause a yearning for the absence of war. Being pulled from the freezing waters in time is a welcome one will never forget.

*Railroad station sign at Werdau, Germany in 1999 —
location of Stalag IV-F, where I was in 1945.*

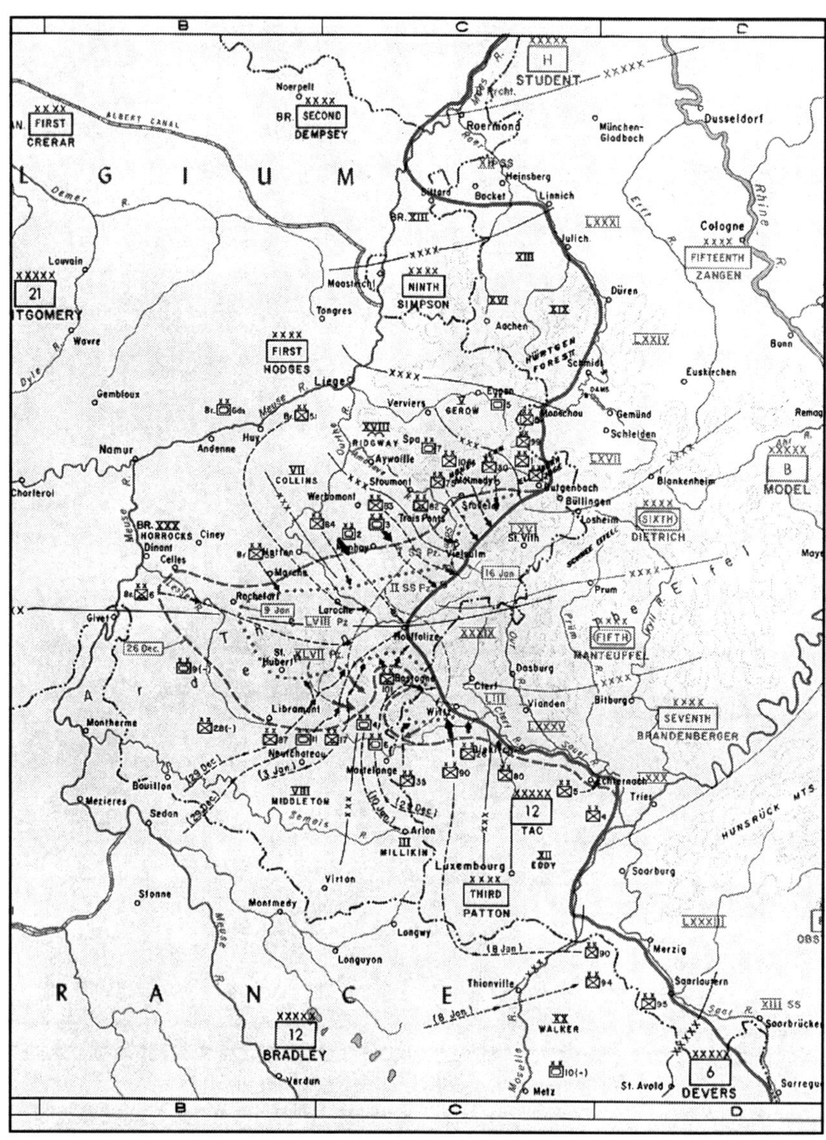

*Map showing order of battle near where Bob Buntin
was in December, 1944.*

Chapter II

"Well alright you damn little fool," I kept repeating to myself, as I clawed my way up a snow-covered Vosges Mountain, New Years Day 1945, about dusk, scared and all alone. The words were of the Blackstone postmaster, my boss, when he gave up trying to talk me out of ending up in the very kind of predicament that I now found myself. (Neither he nor the "damn little fool" had an inkling I would one day succeed him in office.) However, I was in love in 1942 and thought going to war was the most welcome and opportune way possible to prove that love. The words kept ringing in my ears as I slipped, cursed, and shifted my M-1 rifle. The chatter of a German machine gun at the foot of the mountain encouraged my anxious ascent.

Why didn't I listen? "You idiot," to myself. "You thought you knew what war was like! And you didn't have a clue. You damn little fool." Tears filled my eyes as I thought of my mother receiving the telegram of regret. I'm listening to the distant pounding of our artillery and following that sound in hope of reaching our lines. "I wonder who she will marry! You're, going to freeze to death on this mountain. How romantic! God, what am I doing here? How did I get here?"

Our infantry "Charlie" Company, part of the 62nd Armored Infantry Battalion, 14th Armored Division, had been overrun New Year's Eve; part of the Battle of the Bulge. I am now lost in the bitterly cold Vosges Mountains of northeastern France. It was a beautiful but awesome sight, to look out from the downside of one mountain and see nothing in your line of travel but one snow-covered mountain peak after another.

Upon gaining my freedom months later, the debriefing officer for the U.S. Army asked if the date of my missing in action, 01-01-45, and date of capture were the same? When I answered in the negative, he asked for the date of surrender and I gave him, 01-06-45. Upon reflection it must have been about 01-04-45 because the frigid like conditions made it seem longer than it actually was. I simply lost track of time and believe the army's date of record that I gave them is incorrect. I had no timepiece.

What a wonderful thing, to have a war with which to exemplify my love. The two are inextricably intertwined, so I must love war. No, I hate war, the same as everybody else. So, is it the bellicose chief leading his receptive followers into the abyss of war as John Stoessinger contends in his book, *Why Nations Go To War*? He then answers the title of his book, "nations don't go to war men do." Why do you suppose we go so often as we all hate war?

If history could give the cause for the decline of the British Empire with only one word, it would be *war*. It had endured but it had cost too much, too long; too many wars, beginning with the Boer wars.

The old farmhouse where Bob Buntin was born in the St. Marks area of Nottoway County, Virginia. The most prominent figure on the steps is his half-brother, Fred Dillemuth.

Chapter III

"There never was a time when, some way could not be found to prevent the drawing of the sword." – Ulysses S. Grant

"Never think that war, no matter how necessary, nor how justified, is not a crime." – Ernest Hemingway

There were more desertions and resulting executions in the Civil War than any war before or since. The Union Army suffered the most with one out of every seven deserting (about 200,000 deserters) and the Confederate Army, one out of every nine or (about 104,000). The problem impacted the South the most because there were a half million fewer men under arms. There were three sided formations for required witnessing of the executions to discourage the shameful death, and die the good death in battle. These formal executions for many, were a hard thing to take.

During World War II, while planning the invasion of Sicily with his staff, the great General George S.

Patton, Jr. blurted out, "God, how I love war!" There were other times in which Patton, upon witnessing the aftermath of violence and the bloody gore of war, expressed his love of war.

It is quite a presumption to think you know something about love and war, which has not already been written. Listen to the words of Otto Rank, the great psychoanalyst: "For the time being I gave up writing – there is already too much truth in the world – an overproduction which apparently cannot be consumed." Nevertheless there is a compulsion to write on, if blissfully, as there is nothing more important in the world than to seek peace, the absence of war. "Blessed are the peacemakers for they shall be called the sons of God."

Love is a many "splendored" – "splintered" thing! I will speak to love mostly in the abstract, but how all kinds of love are intertwined with war. Why do two people in love let war interfere and destroy their relationship? The consummation of their love becomes dependent upon the personal need to go to war. The conclusion drawn is that man loves war in order that he may have a realization of love.

War is the means whereby he is able to exhibit and prove his undying love! This is the ultimate in our thinking, to risk dying for the one we love by going off to war. How else can I prove my love, but to fight for you, for country! I'm not worthy of your love if I do otherwise. No amount of pleading is sufficient to keep me from going. It is the only way to prove, to justify that love – to join with others, to go to war.

It is compelling and there is no way out, but why do I want to risk losing that which I love by going to war? Is it egotistical insanity? Maybe in part, but it is also about heroics, and belief in one's immortality. We think we're indestructible, which has to do with being so young and naïve.

I'm exempt from the draft but must go in order to prove that love, and return the hero. I shall survive the mortality of the bullet for I am indestructible.

It's all about luck! Though I sense my number coming up, my own mortality remains unreal. The denial of death is essential in order to cope with its realization.

Andy Rooney, former (combat) war correspondent during WW II, and now of *60 Minutes* fame, proclaimed, "I do not accept the inevitability of my own death. I secretly think there may be some other way out."

Chapter IV

The public relations media of WW II, or the propaganda media seemed to be directed right at me, and this was such a patriotic time. It was a must that we pull together in order to win the war. The newscasts made you want to serve your country, to want to be in uniform, making you feel guilty if you were not. I was exempt from the draft because I was the only means of support for my widowed mother, my father having died when I was nine. This did not lessen the youthful desire to serve, to do my duty, the same as friends already gone to war. And when a Jewish high school friend who had volunteered for the paratroopers was killed, that was the last straw. I had to go!

I was a senior in high school when I fell in love. Now, I needed to display to the love of my life, my manhood by being willing to die for her and country. In June of 1942, Pearl Harbor was more than six months old, and that October when I turned eighteen, I registered for the draft.

This is a clear case of how romantic love is intertwined with war. It is the ultimate means whereby I am able to show, to prove my love, by willing to die for her love. Yes, willing, but not believing. I shall return from the war the hero, to claim my love. However, I am not a hero after all, because if I'm immortal, as I believe, I cannot become the real hero.

The song, "As Time Goes By" tells it well.

It's still the same old story,
a fight for love and glory,
a case of do or die,
the world will always welcome lovers,
as time goes by.

George Garrett, author of *The Death of a Fox* has it this way: "Peace is so high prized because there's damn little of it. In truth there is none and never has been, not since we were drummed out of Eden. Even in peacetime there's always murder and war in men's hearts. The world with all its history, knowledge, and contrary evidence, has always believed that men fight and die best for a good cause and do not die well in the service of wickedness. Such is to allow any old soldier in hearing distance to laugh out loud! The cause for being where he is, that's the first thing a soldier discards to lighten his marching load. His only cause is to live as long as he can. And sometimes he must fight very well for that cause. Soldiers know there was, is, never shall be, any cause or purpose worth dying for. They die when they have to and as well as they can. And that's the first secret of the soldier's craft. All wars and fights are the same and all soldiers the same. But by the same rule, every soldier is single and unique. To be a good soldier is to be drunk on what's here – a pair of dry socks, birdcalls from a bush, clear water, a bottle of wine, the body of a woman." Am I wrong with Garrett's contradiction? Love is worth dying for and my very reason for going to war. Love and War are inextricably intertwined!

Man continues to delude himself in claiming and proclaiming how he hates war. Of all the worthwhile charities and causes we pursue there are none more worthy than the search for peace. The following is one historical example of man's love for war. There was the slightest chance that World War I could be averted. But why not! A win, is a win, is a win, and one man (one person) had it in his power to prevent the calamity.

The urgent telegrams went out that there was the possibility of a last minute diplomatic solution. The order had been issued and there were eleven thousand trains rushing towards the border of Luxembourg that would set off the war. The German Chief of Staff (for the love of God?) burst into tears of abject despair, and thought his heart would break. His vision of eleven thousand trains being wrenched into reverse was too much for him to bear, and he refused to honor and countermand the order. The invasion of Luxembourg had begun and so had World War I. "Nations don't go to war, men do."

There was not a single nation, which began a war in the twentieth century that emerged a winner.

Therefore, there was not a single man starting a war in the twentieth century who emerged a winner. These are echoes emanating out of Iraq and Afghanistan today, had we only listened and heeded this subtle piece of history. It appears at this writing, after over nine years in Afghanistan, we are setting a time frame to pull out. After over eight years in Iraq, we have finally begun bringing our fighting men home from that misconceived escapade. (Nations don't go to war, men do.) We can claim no victory from either war, maybe a face-saving humanitarian success, if that. Echoes from the past keep ringing in our ears. History reveals that it is the continuity of war, which brings about the decline of nations, of empires. Can we find a long respite from war?

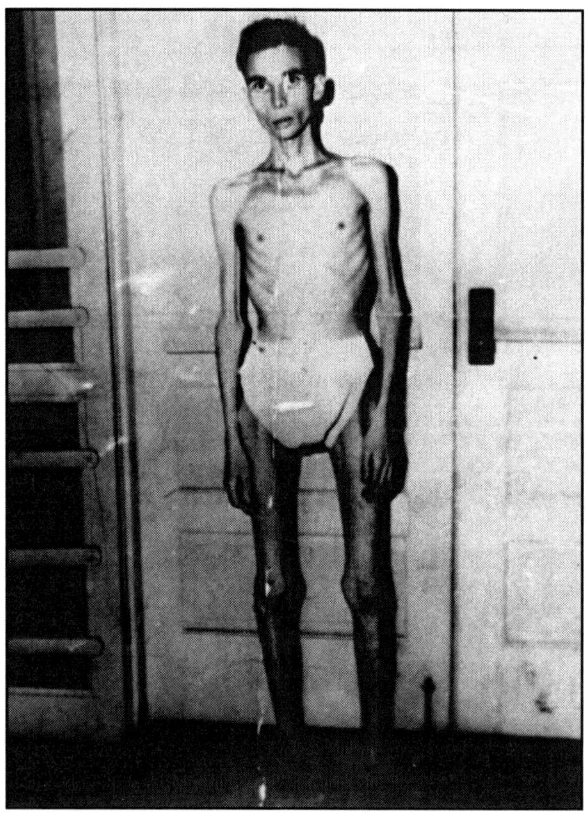

Physique of a GI upon release from a German POW Camp, WW-II.

Bob Buntin weighed 160 pounds when captured and 95 pounds upon liberation.

Chapter V

There was at least one member of the Blackstone Jaycees (USJCOC) who disagreed with the second line of the creed, which is: "That the brotherhood of man transcends the sovereignty of nations." This was the only line of this otherwise magnificent creed, which created doubt, because of the implied meaning of our willingness to surrender our country's sovereignty for brotherly love. We recited our national creed in unison at all of our meetings, and continued to do so, even after the line in question was brought to the attention of the full body. This was something dangerous for us to believe, that we would give up our sovereignty for any cause. There can be nothing, of course, which can transcend the sovereignty of our nation! The valid point of objection never deterred us from continuing with the recitation of our creed. It was concluded that it has the meaning of good will towards man, nothing more.

The complete creed is:

We believe:

That faith in God gives meaning and purpose to human life;

That the brotherhood of man transcends the sovereignty of nations;

That economic justice can best be won by free men through free enterprise;

That government should be of laws rather than of men;

That earths great treasure lies in human personality;

And that service to humanity is the best work of life."

Corporal Adolf Hitler became a German hero in World War I, awarded just about every combat medal the German government could offer, including the Iron Cross First Class. He was wounded and gassed in battle. The lowly ranked corporal, bowing to the generals in World War I, would have the generals bowing to him in World War II.

It can be argued that he was a believer in "brotherly love," but his belief rested upon the premise that such love be assigned only to a pure racial kind of brother. *Mein Kampf*, translated *My Struggle*, in one sense was his revelation to the world of his future intentions. Konrad Heiden in his introduction to *Mein Kampf* gives us something to think about now.

"For years, *Mein Kampf* stood as proof of the blindness and complacency of the world. For in its pages, Hitler announced – long before he came to power – a program of blood and terror in a self-revelation of such overwhelming frankness that few among its readers had the courage to believe it. Once again, it was demonstrated that there was no more effective method of concealment than the broadest publicity…That such a man could go so far toward realizing his ambitions, and – above all – could find millions of willing tools and helpers; that is a phenomenon the world will ponder for centuries to come."

This was the herd instinct following the dangerous personality that many of the world's leading psychoanalysts had warned about years before Hitler. How relevant is this to our world today? Not Nazism, but some other kind of group formation with an idealism, which it wishes to force upon the world. "Nations don't go to war men do."

Ayn Rand's book, *The Ominous Parallels*, sheds a remarkable insight for all of us. The how of Hitler's Germany coming into being is revealed with such thoroughness it scares you. It scares because of the way she compares it with a similar trend today. In summary, it is the gradual, or not so gradual, erosion of individual freedoms. Individualism gave way to statism in pre-war Germany in much the same way we have become more of a welfare state today. It is no longer the individual laboring for his own benefit so much as laboring for the welfare state. He is enabled thereby to keep his job, and contribute to the welfare state, supporting the trend towards statism, "a system where the economy is regulated by the State."

For example, there is the relatively recent seat belt law, which has proven to save lives and prevent serious injuries. It is a good law, being so beneficial to society at large, but just an example of another small loss of individual freedom, the right to buckle up, or not to buckle up.

This means, for better or worse, we are becoming more and more, a democracy rather than a republic. Ironic is it not, that our hope is that democracy wins over in other countries? According to most students of government and history, our founding fathers' intention was a republic; and it is now slipping away. The individual is, or was, primary, whereas more control of our lives is being passed to the state.

What, if anything, is it that we can do to keep us a

republic, or do we want to? Is our trend towards statism, already unstoppable – or do we want to stop it? Do we want to reinstate our founding fathers' republic, and a return to individualism?

In 1787, at the conclusion of the Constitutional Convention, when asked what kind of government the framers were giving to the new nation, Benjamin Franklin answered: "A Republic, if you can keep it."

Bob Buntin returns to Germany and France where he fought during World War II. Here he is looking at the Zwickau Railway Station in 1999.

Chapter VI

The likelihood of us becoming a dictatorship is highly unlikely but what kind of national government is most likely to keep us out of war? It doesn't matter, if we are to believe Stosseinger, in his book, *Why Nations Go To War.* We need not discuss political forms of government such as more a democracy and less a republic, or socialism versus capitalism. We wish to address here what kind of leader is most likely to keep us out of war. We want someone leading us, when war is all but inevitable, to abolish the inevitable. There must be no such thing as the inevitable when it comes to going to war. It's as simple as that! War and all the misery it brings is too horrible to comprehend, until we find ourselves on the battleground. And it is not only the soldier's battleground of misery and terror but more than ever a civilian battleground of misery and terror.

The biblical contention that there will always be war and rumors of war is as wrong as other literal interpretations of the Bible. The major issues that we face to keep from going to war are many-fold, but the basic problem, as heretofore stated, is our love of war. The slogan, "freedom is not cheap" is a truism that we pay with our life for the freedom we enjoy. There is the implication that war and its ultimate price is the only means we have of realizing freedom. This is a concept that we can and must reject.

The wrong-headedness is that we must show and prove love of our mate through love of a fight, a love of war. It's about competition as reflected in many lower animals and the various means they have of attracting their mates. More often than not there is the fight, the necessary macho demonstration, to strut, to frighten, to fight off the competition, in order to win over one's mate. While we are at the top of the chain, the human animal, we are still animal, lest we forget. Must we continue to strut and fight, in order to truly love? Does this explain our love for war and the answer of why we go so often? Or, is it the innate, unchangeable nature of man?

The answer my friend is blowin' in the wind.

Chapter VII

There we were, "Charlie" Company caught in the open, with no place to hide and no time to dig foxholes. The Germans' deadly accurate 88 artillery shells had already killed and wounded a number of men. We had been exchanging rifle and machine gun fire, off and on, with dug-in German infantry for an hour or more. Word was passed down to keep the wounded quiet, that they were going to give away our position. How do you keep people quiet in the throes of pain and dying! You can't, the only way to quiet the moaning and screaming was to find a medic with morphine. The trouble was finding one who was not wounded himself, or not already administering first aid to someone. I cite this minor skirmish, major for those of us there, as another example of the horror of war.

I had volunteered to go with my squad leader, Bob Montgomery, on a recon patrol this beautiful night (11-27-44) near the town of Benfeld, France. We had been leapfrogging each other heading towards enemy lines when the earth suddenly erupted around us. I think I have always resented not getting wounded more seriously so I could go home with Montgomery. He was seriously wounded and was removed from all the Hell, leaving me to continue to contend with it. Also, my best friend in the squad, Ralph Livoni, got hit the same night, and escaped from all the bloody gore and misery of war. It was sometime later, in the Battle of the Bulge, when I became a casualty, a prisoner of war. I wanted to go home to my loved ones, like Montgomery and Livoni, to a hero's welcome, to find my love in waiting. That was not to be. I had to continue to endure.

We, as individuals, and as sovereign nations, it seems, would have become by now, more civil, less aggressive, and more considerate of our fellow man. Yet as we discovered as recently as World War II, with the murder and treatment of the Jews, as well as other groups and individuals, we have a long way to go.

One would think, as sophisticated as we are, with the new technology, with our new knowledge of the humanities, that we would have more compassion towards our fellow man. Why, do you think, we continue to war, to murder, just as awful, all the way back to biblical times? Is it about economics, the geographical divide, the continued struggle between the haves and the have-nots? This has been the rationale or the enlisted cause of war for too long. The economic consideration is only part of the reason calling for war. Man loves to fight, to war. We simply contradict the claim of our hatred of war!

There is at least some effort, some demonstration, to share our goods, our good geographical fortune and welfare with others. Then we have leaders and groups who want to war, and they bring us along, as though we were captive, to join in their war. Could it be that simple, that so many of us are tempted to follow and just love war? We teach love, and preach love, and make love, and profess love, and then we go to war, because of what? Love! We love to war, in order to love, and we must war, as our means to prove that love. What a state of contradictions! Is there the slightest chance of ever abolishing war, which supposedly we hate, and retain love?

The answer my friend is blowin' in the wind.

It has been suggested by some students of history, as well as students on the subject addressed here, that our bellicose inclination comes from the founding of our country. We justly rebelled, and became a lingering by-product of war, resulting from the Revolutionary War. Could this be an inkling of truth, because of our beginning, that we are more inclined to find ourselves involved in conflicts, in warring, wisely or unwisely? Do our leaders still wear the warriors' uniform upon which our nation came in to being? What foolish rationale some would say that our going to war so often, has anything to do with our war founded existence. We hate war! We only war to defend ourselves, or defend others, and then only because it's in our national interest.

I am not a pacifist! I wanted to go to war, and chose to go because I loved the opportunity that war allowed me, to prove my love. Therefore I am a hawk who loves war, cause and effect too factual to ignore. Rushing forth again come the lyrics, *"it's still the same old story, a fight for love and glory, a case of do or die."* Oh, so love and war is the combination we could die for? Why, of course!

Lt. Waverly Wray, at dawn on D-Day plus one, headed out into the unknown on a one-man reconnaissance to formulate a plan of attack. He moved through hedgerows, crawled up a ditch crossing an orchard and down sunken lanes. He noted a concentration of Germans in fields and lanes. A man (such as myself) without Wray's woodsman's sense of directions would have gotten lost. Wray, moving like the deer stalker he was, got to a place where he could hear guttural voices on the other side of a hedgerow. They sounded like officers talking about map coordinates.

Wray burst through the hedgerow, swung his M-1 to a ready position and barked out in his powerful command voice, *"Hande hoch!"* to the eight German officers gathered around a radio.

Seven instinctively raised their hands. The eighth tried to pull a pistol from his holster. Wray shot him in an instant between the eyes. He dropped to his knee and shot the other seven officers in the head as they attempted to run away. Two Germans, in a slit trench some distance behind him opened fire with their Schmeisser machine pistols. One bullet cut off half of his right ear. Others cut through his jacket, miraculously missing him. Wray jumped into a ditch, putting a new clip in his M-1. He killed the two Germans with the Schmeissers with one shot to the head of each.

Wray made his way back to the company area to report on what he had seen and get himself patched up. He would then lead the company in an attack down one of the lanes. The six thousand Germans poised to attack, having been left leaderless by Wray, broke and ran. Thanks mainly to a one-man reconnaissance in the person of Lt. Waverly Wray. By mid-morning, the potential for a German breakthrough to the beaches was greatly diminished.

Wray was a big man, 250 pounds, with legs like tree trunks. The standard army issue parachute wasn't large enough, as he dropped too fast in his jumps. His men joked, "Hell, with legs like that, he don't need a chute." Colonel Ben Vanderwoort, commander of the 505th Parachute Infantry, 82nd Airborne Division said, "Wray was as experienced and skilled as an infantry soldier can get and still be alive."

Wray, from Batesville, Mississippi, had Deep South religious convictions. A Baptist, each month he sent half his pay home to help build a new church. He never swore, didn't drink, smoke, or chase after girls. Some troopers called him the Deacon, but in the admiring kind of way. When exasperated, his primary exclamation was "John Brown" referring to the abolitionist of

Harpers Ferry. Much later, during the ill-conceived and unnecessary operation, "Market Garden," in the Netherlands, a German sniper got Wray between the eyes as he raised his head to look over the situation.

He loved his country and had what it takes to win battles, while living an exemplary life. Did he love war? Who knows? Duty, honor, valor!

Bob's uniform from WWII including his corporal's stripes, Combat Infantryman's Badge (awarded only for actual ground combat), Bronze Star (Army's 4th highest medal), the POW Medal, the Purple Heart (recieved for suffering wounds in combat), the French Medal of Freedom.

Chapter VIII

There are those who claim we are a Christian nation, that our founding fathers were Christian. We subscribe to the great teachings of Jesus, "love thy neighbor as thyself," and that applies to nations as well as individuals. The theory being that, as Christians, we would less likely go to war.

However, there are students of history and government who contend our founders were not Christian. There is documentation that many of the early presidents and patriots were not Christians and were either Deists or Unitarians. They believed in some form of impersonal Providence, but rejected the divinity of Jesus, and the absurdities of the Old and New Testaments.

Thomas Paine was one whose manifestos encouraged the faltering spirits of the country and aided materially in winning the war of Independence. "I do not believe in the creed professed by the Jewish church, by the Roman church, by the Greek church, by the Turkish church, by the Protestant church, nor by any church that I know of … Each of those churches accuse the other of unbelief; and for my own part, I disbelieve them all." (From: *The Age of Reason* by Thomas Paine)

I believe churches do much good, but I am also a strong believer in the separation of church and state. I would not want Christianity, or any other religion, to be a part of government with undue influence on governmental policies. There is too much history of religious wars to wish for that; and would open up the potential for political abuse based on religious belief.

George Washington, our first president, never declared himself a Christian in any of his voluminous correspondence. He championed the cause of freedom from intolerance of all religions. On his deathbed, Washington uttered no words of a religious nature and did not ask for a clergyman. (From: *George Washington and Religion* by Paul F. Boller, Jr.)

John Adams, the country's second president, remarked that he found among the clergy, "the pretended sanctity of some absolute dunces." Also, "This would be the best of all possible worlds, if there were no religion in it." It was during Adams' administration that the Senate ratified the Treaty of Peace and Friendship, which states in Article XI "the government of the United States of America is not in any sense founded on the Christian Religion." (From: *The Character of John Adams* by Peter Shaw)

Thomas Jefferson, the third president and author of the Declaration of Independence, referred to the Revelation of St. John as "the ravings of a maniac." He also said, "I trust that there is not a young man now living in the United States who will not die a Unitarian." He implied from his writings, the disbelief of the story of Jesus, citing the inexplicable Platonisms associated with it. (From: *Thomas Jefferson, an Intimate History* by Fawn M. Brodie)

James Madison, our fourth president and father of the Constitution was not religious in any conventional sense. "Religious bondage shackles and debilitates the mind and unfits it for every noble enterprise." (From: *The Madisons* by Virginia Moore)

Ethan Allen, commander of the Green Mountain Boys, at the capture of Fort Ticonderoga, helped inspire Congress and the country to pursue the War of Independence. Allen, a Deist, said, "That Jesus Christ was not God is evidence from his own words."

(From: *Religion of the American Enlightenment* by G. Adolph Koch)

Historians consider Benjamin Franklin, like so many great Americans of his time, to be a Deist, not a Christian. (From: *Benjamin Franklin, A Biography in his Own Words* edited by Thomas Fleming)

Do we want to draw a conclusion that our Founding Fathers, not being of the Christian persuasion, loved war more? Not for a minute! Faith has nothing to do with our love of war and why we go so often. It is more likely the innate nature of man.

> *The Moving Finger writes; And having writ,*
> *Moves on: nor all thy Piety nor Wit*
> *Shall lure it back to cancel half a Line,*
> *Nor all thy Tears wash out a Word of it.*
> *—Omar Khayyam*

Chapter IX

Would the recitation of more blood and gore help to urge us on, into the twilight, in the quest for the abandonment of war? I meet with my friend, Mac Williams, along with others, for coffee almost every morning in historic downtown Blackstone. Mac was in the first wave of Marines landing on the beaches of Iwo Jima in World War II, and about all we ever hear him say is, "I have been pretty lucky." What an understatement, but that's what it is, just luck! Mac who is now 88 is very modest and humbled by his experiences.

He had been wounded earlier in another one of the invasions of Japanese held islands; and another time, miraculously survived his ship blowing up, and being pulled from the Pacific waters. He fought the ferocious, non-surrendering Japanese close up and personal, and survived, while many of his friends, right beside him did not. It takes one of unusually strong character not to be affected in some way by his kind of experience. Mac, outwardly, gives no sign of war's effect, but inwardly, we can only guess. For example, a GI fighting in Italy in WW II shot a German close up in the face with his 45, and says he has shot that German a thousand times in his dreams.

Then I have my own dreams sometimes, bad dreams or nightmares about the war. I seldom sleep in the same bed with my wife, June, anymore. I guess she has gotten tired of me kicking her, though she hardly complains when I do. I sleep in a recliner most of the time now, mainly because it is more comfortable with a back/neck problem. I had an old quart-size jar of marbles for a paperweight on the small table by my recliner. It was about three-fourths full and I enjoyed looking at the bright and colorful marbles of all different sizes.

I was fighting the other night, flailing and crawling away from an artillery barrage of German 88 shells. There was a mighty explosion. I bolted upright to find to my relief it was only a dream. I had knocked the jar of marbles off the table with an explosion like crash, glass marbles and broken glass everywhere. It was loud, awakening my wife in a room some distance from me. She came at three o'clock in the morning to help clean up the mess and in good humor, observed, "I thought you had already lost all your marbles!"

War is Hell! Whatever Hell is, it is our way of describing how bad or terrible something is. The Bible speaks of Hell in the hereafter, but I don't believe in such a thing. Hell is right here on earth, and often enough, for many, life is a living Hell! Then, if Hell is here on earth, so is Heaven, whatever that is, but is our way of describing how good something is. Therefore, Man must love Hell because he loves War; and the infantryman's Heaven is a pair of dry socks, a bottle of wine, and the body of a woman.

Audie Murphy's book, *To HELL and BACK* is, by its very title, helpful in describing what war is like in the infantry, and why war is synonymous with hell. The most decorated soldier of WW II, including the Medal of Honor, speaks in his book of demons. Following one of his close and personal combat experiences, he describes it: "I remember the experience as I do a nightmare. A demon seems to have entered my body. My brain is coldly alert and logical. I do not think of the danger to myself. My whole being is concentrated on killing."

Audie Murphy suffered from what we know today as post-traumatic stress disorder. The World War II disorder was characterized as "Battle Fatigue." In

World War I it was known as "Shell Shocked." A deranged Audie Murphy once held his wife hostage, at gunpoint.

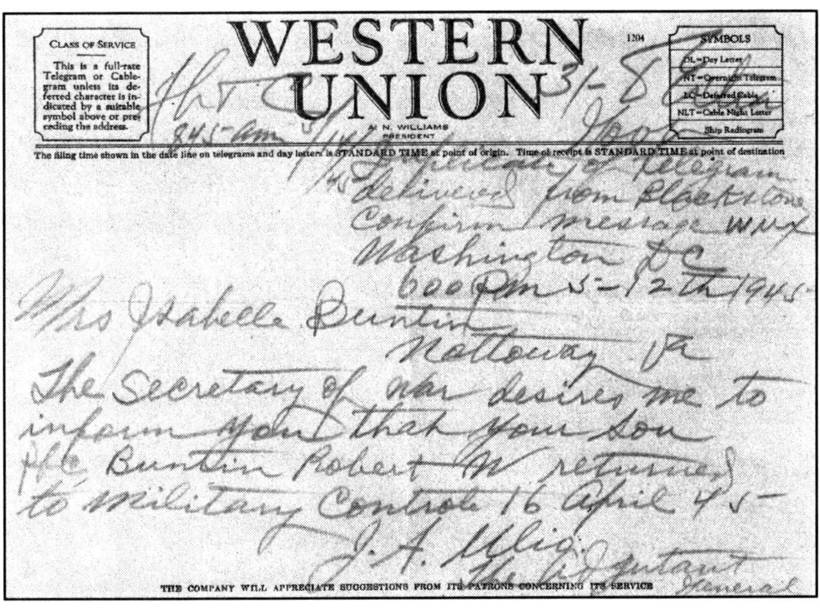

*Telegram sent in **1945** from the Secretary of War reporting Bob's release from captivity.*

Chapter X

Fumio Tamamura was born in San Francisco and now lives in Yokohama, Japan. He was a Japanese soldier and in 1945 was stationed on Chichi Jima, a small island adjacent to Iwo Jima. This small Japanese owned island was being used for monitoring American movements in WW II with an elaborate radio station for sending and receiving messages. It was manned by a small Japanese force – with expertise in radio operations. The small island, generally uninhabited, was considered a part of the Japanese homeland, the same as next-door Iwo Jima.

Fumio Tamamura, in the war year 1945, walked James Wesley (Jimmy) Dye, Jr. to his death on Chichi Jima, where he was beheaded. Today, Tamamura is a member of Rotary International which strikes me as somewhat ironic while writing this, that I am a member of the same. Tamamura must be at least in his late eighties or nineties, and is respected by his acceptance into Rotary International. George Herbert

Walker Bush (41st president of the United States), while piloting his bomber near Chichi Jima was shot down. We are all familiar with the story of his rescue by a nearby American submarine. Our president to be, fortunately snatched from the Pacific waters by our sub, was far enough from the shores of Chichi Jima, not to be rescued by the Japanese stationed there. The enemy in a small boat launched from Chichi Jima, was too far away to rescue the downed airman, thank goodness. There were eight other American airmen around this same time in 1945, shot down near the island. They were not so fortunate, were captured and became prisoners of war there.

James Bradley's book, *Flyboys*, reveals for the first time the fate of these eight Americans who simply disappeared for decades, even after the end of WW II. Bradley's book also shows the ruthlessness, the inhumanity of man, caused by war. All is fair in love and war rings true to the word, "ALL." *War is Hell* is one of the most understated descriptions of war anyone can conjure up.

These young men were carried by our military as missing in action (MIA) for such a long time, and we can only guess how trying this must have been for their loved ones. It took James Bradley's untiring research, and visiting Chichi Jima with President George H. W. Bush, to finally bring the plight of these American airmen (POWs) to our attention.

Tom Hanks, in his production of the televised documentary *The Pacific*, wants us to understand the iniquities as well as the glories of war. He portrays well the bravery, the misery, and the difficulty of our troops fighting the entrenched, ferocious Japanese. He also wants Americans today, to reflect and say, "We didn't know our troops did that to the Japanese."

He doesn't see the ten-hour series as simply eye-opening history. He wants us to ponder the sacrifices of our current soldiers in Iraq and Afghanistan, but he also wants to make people wonder how our troops can reenter society in the first place. How can they just pick up where they left off? Things moved slower in WW II. Soldiers had more time to decompress, returning on ships, then time across country by train, allowing more time for adjusting. Today, combatants are flown back home in eighteen hours, and expected to fit right in again! He thinks that is unrealistic.

"We viewed the Japanese as 'yellow slant-eyed dogs' that believed in different gods. They were out to kill us because our way of living was different. We, in turn, wanted to annihilate them because they were different." He poses the question, "does that sound familiar today?"

The great hope is that sooner rather than later, we become weary enough of war that once again war cures itself. Our state of continual warfare will surely and certainly become our downfall, no longer "The Super Power" of the world.

The same clock still hung in Werdau Railway station in 1999 as I also saw in 1945.

Chapter XI

These eight American airmen may have thought themselves safe upon surviving their stricken (shot down) airplanes and becoming POWs. They may have been unaware that Japan was not a signatory to the Geneva Convention and the treatment of captured combatants. They may not have been aware of the Japanese culture as well, whereby it was a dishonor to become a prisoner of war.

It was not uncommon for the Japanese to commit suicide rather than surrender or fall into the hands of their enemy. Nevertheless, though relatively few, some became prisoners of war of the United States during WW II. And, some Americans, though harshly treated by the Japanese during their captivity were allowed to survive, but just barely. The well-known philosopher, Immanuel Kant, said: "With men the normal state of nature is not peace but war." The ubiquitous question, can that state of nature ever become a peaceful nature?

All of our airmen on Chichi Jima were beheaded, or otherwise executed, some ceremoniously, with their liver extracted, grilled, and eaten by their Japanese captors. The act of cannibalism was done, supposedly, to enhance the killing spirit of the participating soldier. It is difficult to believe that Japanese officers ordered this act of cannibalism and had portions of the liver served to them by enlisted personnel. Can you believe this occurred in our civilized 20th century? It is difficult to comprehend, but something we must know, that it may never happen, again. When and where have we heard those words before?

We generally think of being beheaded, as a swift and expertly administered kind of death. This is not always the case. A reluctant Japanese soldier upon being ordered by his superiors to perform an execution, wielding an unsteady sword, botched the execution. The American airman, kneeling with his hands tied behind his back, coped with his tortuous death as best he could.

There's documented evidence of more blood and gore on Chichi Jima. The Japanese in charge there wanted to instill the killer instinct, to make better warriors of some of the rank and file members. They had two of the captured American airmen bound and tied to well constructed stakes, then painted large circles around the heart area of each, and made ready for live bayonet practice. The orders for the Japanese soldiers were to charge with fixed bayonets, to thrust the bayonet to a part of the body of their own choosing, except for the circled part. This would cause our airmen to linger longer, and suffer more, as punishment for their bombing runs on Chichi Jima and Iwo Jima. The exercise would, explained their superiors, serve to remove squeamishness from their otherwise well trained warriors.

Isn't war hell! Well, at least they didn't burn them at the stake!

Chapter XII

The most tragic war for our country in so many ways was the Civil War, with brother killing brother. There has been since the ending of that slaughter and suffering, one conflict after another, with only small intervals of that highly prized peace. Will it ever end?

"Yes we can!" President Obama's campaign slogan rings hollow as we approach the second anniversary of his election. The attack on us by hoodlums, (09/11/01) killing thousands, sent us to war in Iraq. We continue to look for that "needle in a haystack" and our war in Afghanistan is extended.

We love to fight, to war, while declaring our hatred of the same. Studying war and how to war (sorry, how to defend ourselves) is our all consuming endeavor and concern. It is responsible for the major portion of our national debt. We are in danger of defeating ourselves from within, with the strain on our financial system. And our collapse would trigger a global collapse, plunging us, and the world into another Great

Depression. We spend so much of our resources preparing for war, (for defense) that we can't afford a war on poverty, arguably the primary cause of war.

In 2008 we spent three trillion dollars or about twenty percent of our gross domestic product (GDP) on defense. This has been the case for over a decade with about one-fifth of our GDP going for defense. Whoever proposes even a small reduction in defense spending is roundly criticized for being weak on national security. Whether it is wise or unwise, and no matter who is President/Commander In-Chief, the party in power, with any proposal for a reduction in defense spending, is tantamount to committing political suicide.

How many military oriented institutions of higher learning do we have? And good ones too! What an honor to be accepted to study at West Point, or the Naval Academy, or the Air Force Academy. It is to their credit that they also turn out people who pursue careers outside of the military field. Nevertheless, their primary purpose of being is the study of war, turning out the best, to lead us into battle. We have many other fine institutions devoted to the same. There is Virginia Military Institute (VMI) which some call the West Point of the South. Let's not forget; how could we,

The Citadel of South Carolina, another fine military school turning out more good military officers.

How many institutions of higher learning do we have studying peace as their primary purpose of existence? I submit the question in jest because I know of none. (I hope no one answers that the schools mentioned are in essence studying peace, defense of our nation).

We have the Peace Corps, but that's not an institution of higher learning. Founded by President John F. Kennedy, who was assassinated, it continues today to do good works in the cause of peace. We had the League of Nations, founded following World War I, the bloodiest war of all. Following World War II, we formed the United Nations. Who can refute their good will effort in the cause of peace?

The Christian religion and other religions also help in the cause of peace. However, how many wars have been waged, fought in the name of, and/or, because of religion? Thomas Jefferson once remarked, "Sometimes I think we would be better off without any religions." A reading of the Crusades chills one to the bone! Man hates war and then is seduced by his love for it. Oh for the whims of man!

*A German guard tower like the one at Stalag IV-B
near Muhlberg, Germany.*

*The remains of the inside wall of the basement of our
Stalag compound, picture taken in 1999. The Stalag
in which we were imprisoned was demolished many
years prior to this photograph.*

Chapter XIII

"It was sheer technical stupidity," it was later determined and decried. Between January and May of 1944 during the Battle of Monte Cassino, our leaders decided to bomb the monastery, The Abbey of Montecassino. There was considerable debate within our own military command, and the Allied command as well, whether to bomb it. The bombers won out over the anti-bombers, and on the 15th of February 1944, our bombers pulverized the historic structure.

We thought the Germans were utilizing it as an observation and operations center. It was being used as a refuge for women and children. There are so many blunders in war. Friendly fire, all too often, takes its dreadful toll. There is nothing, which is immune to destruction and devastation.

A young friend, Bob Quicke, on his way home from work, would often stop by to see me. Bob was president of Southside Transportation Company here in Blackstone, and was also on the Virginia Transportation Board.

We had good enjoyable discussions about local and world affairs, not always agreeing with each other. We always inquired of each other's health, made light talk about our golf game and other things.

One evening upon my inquiring about how he was doing, he said, "I'm seeking peace."

The conversation went something like this: "You know there's no such thing, but what kind of peace?"

"Inner peace."

"What is that?"

"I'm not really sure."

I asked if it had anything to do with world peace, or the lack thereof, causing you to look inside for something?

"Let's not get too deep!"

"How about another martini!"

Thereafter, it became a habit in jest every time we met, "Have you found it yet?"

"I'm still looking."

This was some time before he became ill, and was diagnosed with terminal cancer. It has been almost ten years since his passing. Upon reflection, I too am looking for that indescribable inner peace of which he spoke.

A few days following the bombing and combat in the Battle of Monte Cassino, a group of infantry replacements, direct from basic training in the States, arrived for combat. An American officer charged with assigning them to the respective units, later remarked. "There were these kids with quick smiles, trying to hide their fear and anxiety, and it was all I could do to keep from breaking out in tears, right in front of them."

It is my guess the officer was likely a West Point graduate, who having experienced his own realization of war, found anything but a love for it. He could readily empathize and sympathize with the innocence of these youths who were about to enter into a world of Hell.

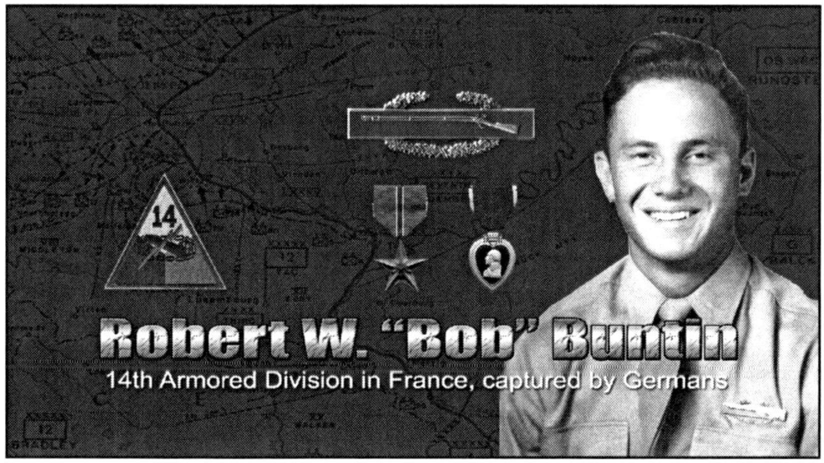

Title screen from 2008 documentary about Bob Buntin's WWII service (American POWs: Men of Steel in Cages of Bamboo and Iron series, 1VIDeo Productions).

My Unit in World World II

Major General A. C. Smith, 14th Armored Division Commander

Colonel James H. Myers, 62nd AIB (Battalion) Commander

Captain Howard A. Trammell, C Company Commander

Lieutenant Edwin M. Kosik, Platoon Leader

Sgt. Bob Montgomery, Squad Leader, 1ˢᵗ Rifle Squad, 3ʳᵈ Platoon, Company C, 62nd Armored Infantry Battalion, 14th Armored Division

Sgt. Bill Henneman, Asst. Squad Leader

Pvt. Claude Ashby

Pvt. Charles Bailey

Pfc. Adelbert (Bert) Brott[1]

Pfc. Bob Buntin

Pvt. Bob Butler

Pfc. Bill Evans

Pfc. Ralph Livoni

Tec-5 Arnold Lopez

Pvt. Bill Sawyer

Pfc. Gunnard Tast[2]

---

[1] *Brott, upon being promoted and taking over the squad was killed the very same day.*

[2] *Tast, an old man of 35, with a wife and child, died in my arms during a 'Screaming Meemie' attack.*

Chapter XIV

We have made the assumption that man loves war, evidentially, because he goes too often not to. Again, is war nothing more than an affliction, a natural condition of man, over which he has no control? In the words of George Bernard Shaw, "If man is not a moral animal he might as well go shoot himself." How profound, and ironic, as that is exactly what we do, go shoot ourselves!

We were in the rich Alsace area of northeastern France, on the outskirts of a small town when we detected some people working the soil near some wooden barracks. Among those working in the group of peasants, were a few men wearing what looked like black and white striped pajamas. As our halftrack (personnel carrier) drew closer, we could see these people were very thin, emaciated and hollow-eyed looking. Years later, upon returning home and reading about the Holocaust, I realized the uniformed striped workers we had seen that day were concentration camp workers/

victims. We liberated this small compound of forced laborers and other prisoners that 1944 December day, as the German force holding the town had moved back. Our column of tanks and armored vehicles rolled on through leaving other units to occupy and investigate.

It's incredible that there are those in political power today, and others, who question or outright don't believe in the Holocaust. Let this attestation, as though any were needed, be added to the overwhelming evidence of the Holocaust. The estimate of the number of Jews murdered during the WW II period ranges from six to eight million, and an untold number of forced laborers of many nationalities, gypsies, and other unknowns were enslaved and murdered. We can trace and account for the effort to exterminate the Jews to one man, Hitler. The herd followed their chief in the commission of atrocities unthinkable in the twentieth century.

"Nations don't go to war, men do."

Chapter XV

"Dying – annuls the power to kill." – Emily Dickinson

It seems man looks for reasons or excuses to go to war, and he finds reason and excuse enough. When he lives in such abject poverty with no hope of life worth living, he is readily prone to dive into the abyss of war. Why not, with the loss of hope, he has nothing to lose! It may be the only means to improve his lot in life. He thinks war cannot be any worse than his life of poverty and despair. His condition cries out for help. We (man) spend trillions on preparedness for war. Why not spend billions to fight poverty, and possibly the prevention of war. The answer is related to the line in the Jaycee creed, "That the brotherhood of man transcends the sovereignty of nations."

How is man's love for each other and his love of war so intertwined that his love of war wins out? Can it be true that he loves war more than he loves his peace? Is there real truth in those lyrics? *It's still the same old story, a fight for Love and Glory."* The want of Love is found in our need for Glory, and the one is not possible without the other. Therefore the two are so intertwined that the only way to Love is in Glory, founded in War.

I was scared to surrender, and scared not to, in my quest to survive. It turned out the decision was made for me, captured in my sleep (how sweet it is)! I fell into the hands of the enemy, so in fact, I surrendered. Had I been surrendering to the Japanese, more than likely, I would not be here writing about it. The culture of the Japanese at the time of WW II was that it did not believe in surrender, and to do so was a dishonor no matter the circumstances. Yet, there were those who fell into our hands, becoming prisoners of war after all.

The young German soldier is standing over me with his machine pistol in my ribs and yelling, *"Raus, Raus"* (get up, move). I bolted upright, and he backed away, and continued to keep his weapon trained on me. He allowed me to slip on my snow-pack boots before taking me out into the frozen, snow-covered, winter wonderland. "Thank you very much!" Sometimes it pays to be an American, at least relative to being a Russian in this world of wars. Had I been a Russian, he was making his prisoner, he may have made me trade shoes with him, or worse, confiscated the boots and made me walk out barefooted, into the snow. You are at the mercy of your adversary who you have been trying to kill, therefore one never knows what to expect.

Is not brotherly love also intertwined with war? The Germans generally treated their American prisoners better than they did their Russian prisoners in WW II. It didn't matter or seem relevant that we were allies against them. There is nothing like an enemy of old to be the most hated enemy.

I thought I had it rough as a prisoner of war under the Germans, but my experience pales in comparison with prisoners in our Civil War, no matter which side. In the course of that war almost 195,000 Union soldiers became POWs, and of these 30,218 died in southern prisons. There were almost 216,000 Confederate POWs, with 25,976 dying in northern prisons. An inmate of the Civil War observed it was, "the closest existence to a hell on earth."

Neither side could imagine the magnitude and length of the conflict. There was a general feeling that it would last no more than a week or two, only a few weeks at the most. That is a common mistaken belief upon the outset of most wars, that it will be of short duration. Only now, in this nuclear age, may the next one prove to be of such brevity. That will be due to destruction and loss of life too unimaginable, even with the pictures and revelation from our bombs on Hiroshima and Nagasaki in WW II.

There were about 625,000 American soldier fatalities in the Civil War – more, or at least equal to, those dying in the Revolutionary War, the War of 1812, the Mexican War, the Spanish-American War, World War I, World War II, and the Korean War combined. "More trying than to face the battle's rage," a Louisiana soldier felt, was the mourning and suffering of family and friends, caused by his death. His almost instant death and suffering would be over, but the agony of loved ones back home would go on and on. For some life itself was shortened by the loss of hope and a will to just die, such was the feeling of helplessness.

It is a consensus of historians and psychologists that this condition was more prevalent in the Civil War than in our more recent wars. The time frame of hope generally was of greater duration before news from the front reached loved ones, the impact of loss being greater. This applied to both North and South civilian populations.

We are taught to love our enemy, and if we act on that commandment, there must be degrees of love with the example the Germans and Russians set for each other. It follows that hate being the opposite of love the Germans hated us less than their Russian adversary. So there we have degrees of hate just as there are degrees of love.

The intertwining of personal romantic love with war may be more meaningful and understandable than other kinds of love. There are many stories about war being the cause of couples hastening into marriage, as there may be no tomorrow. And, rightly or wrongly, if not marrying, the pleading is usually by the male to let's make love now. I will be gone off to war, never to return, and after all, we love each other. How foolish for two people in love with each other, to think they need war as the means of bonding their love! It must be the nature of man to love war and its irrefutable connection with romantic love!

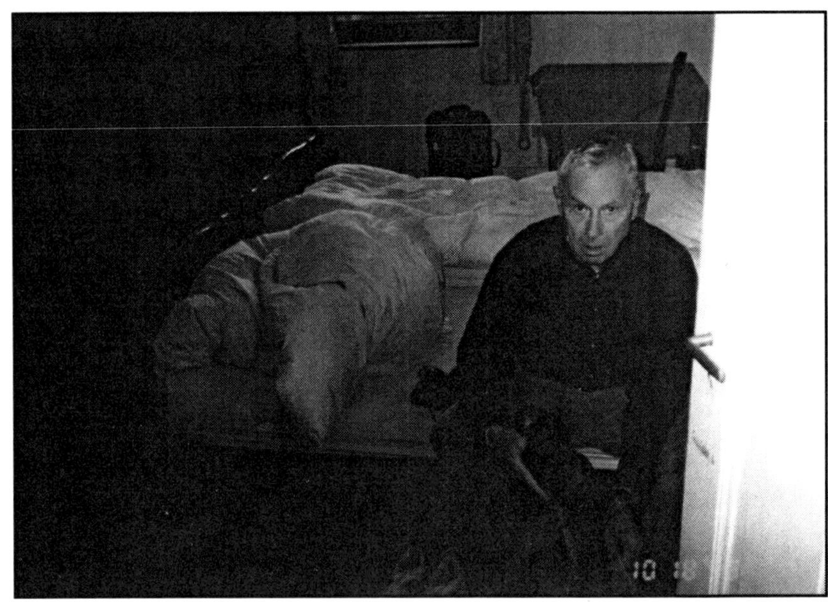

The room in Bannstein, France where Hugh Colbert and I spent the night during our revisit to Europe in 1999. Across from this room, I fired my M1 out of a window on New Year's morning, 1945.

Revisiting battlegrounds with Hugh Colbert in 1999, I found our company commander's old girlfriend!

Chapter XVI

When I enrolled at the College of William and Mary, I was unaware that I was affected by post-traumatic stress disorder. Earlier wars had other names for the same condition. Does war cheapen life, or give one more appreciation for life? I found myself in love with love!

The first thing I did at William and Mary was call up Lucy, who was living in a dorm across the campus from my own dormitory, for a date. The daughter of my former boss, the Blackstone postmaster, she was one good-looking gal. She was one of several reasons I had chosen William and Mary, having decided to give up my old job at the Post Office. I was disappointed and taken aback when she turned me down for a date. She said she was sorry and going steady with Bill, whom she would later marry. However, she offered to get me a date with a friend in her dorm and I immediately accepted the blind date.

A familiar and favorite place of almost every student at William and Mary is the Sunken Gardens, and no less of a favorite for this freshman on his first date. Ruth was of olive complexion with smooth skin and pretty brown eyes. I was so pleased, even awed, at her instant affection. Had Lucy told her friend about my being an ex-prisoner of war, and why she was being so jovial and nice.

We held hands as we strolled across campus to downtown Williamsburg for a Coke before heading back home, or rather to Sunken Gardens. We sat on one of the series of steps above the gardens holding hands, while she talked, with me having little to say. I was just a freshman and she was starting her junior year. Ruth and I would many times, along with groups of friends, stretch out our blankets on the cool green grass under the stars, in the memorable Sunken Gardens.

The good times at William and Mary had nothing to do with me leaving in the middle of my junior year, for they were some of the best times of my life. There were other things bothering me, plus I was drinking heavily, and not learning a great deal. My major was economics with a minor in philosophy. I would later attend Smithdeal-Massey Business College in Richmond, taking courses in typing, business law and accounting.

However, for now, my personal finances needed much healing. Then there was the girl back home who had waited for me to return from the war and I had a guilty conscience upon leaving her again. On a whim, I had to go home. I had to leave William and Mary.

Here with a Loaf of Bread beneath the Bough,
A Flask of Wine, a Book of Verse — and Thou
Beside me singing in the Wilderness —
And Wilderness is Paradise enow.

—Omar Khayyam

Bob Buntin, 2008.

Chapter XVII

What does all this have to do with love and war? I'm searching for love and peace! The only way to love is through war, and our love of war is not understood. My war is over, but the absence of peace remains, and the search for inner peace seems unattainable. Surely we can have love without war. Or is it true, as in *Death of a Fox*, there is no peace, never has been, and never will be? Does the make up of man make peace impossible? The love of war contradicts his claim of seeking peace. How cynical can one be? We find joy in the absence of pain, but no peace in the absence of war.

It is the belief of many accredited psychologists that man would be incapable of passionate love if he knew he would live forever. Would we be willing to give up passionate love should we find a way to live forever? Some say they would be happy with a mediocre kind of love for the privilege of living forever. We may think this way at first, but then find to live without passionate love is not worth living. Passionate love, and passionate sexual intercourse are not the same, though passionate lovemaking can be part of the kind of passion of which the writer speaks. Just what do we mean? It is that indescribable love which transforms one into the very being of another, the two becoming one. Must we have war in order that we may truly love?

The answer my friend is blowin' in the wind.

<u>References Used in Writing This Book</u>

Citizen Soliders, Stephen E. Ambrose

To Hell and Back, Audie Murphy

The Conscience of a Conservative, Barry Goldwater

The Death of a Fox, George Garrett

Why Nations Go to War, John Stoessinger

Mein Kampf, Adolph Hitler

The Ominous Parallels, Ayn Rand

Flyboys, James Bradley

The Pacific, TV documentary, Tom Hanks

Chapter XVIII

To the Virgins, To Make Much of Time

Gather ye rosebuds while ye may,
Old Time is still a-flying:
And this same flower that smiles today,
To-morrow will be dying.
—Robert Herrick

Ruth and I were with two other couples from William and Mary when we stopped by a hotel to look in on some friends we had been with at the ballgame. We were in Richmond. "The Kid," my friend and roommate, John B. Wilson, from Crewe, asked me to go with him to find these people we knew. We left our dates with our other male companion and his date in the car, and said we would be back in a "jiffy," a few minutes.

The year was 1947 and we were all students at William and Mary. I followed the Kid from the hotel desk to the elevator and he was soon rapping on the door of a hotel room. It was a suite of rooms with several people moving about and some loud talking. The Kid went into an adjoining room with a man and two girls I didn't know, closed and locked the door. I was left in the room with Jim, a man we had met at the game, not a William and Mary student, and two non-student girls he had with him at the game.

Jim told me to have a drink, that he had to take one of the girls home (she was standing there with her coat on) and he would be back in a few minutes. Jim's date, who I had just met at the game, was in the bed with the covers pulled up to her chin.

Maggie invited me over almost as soon as Jim was out the door, one bare white arm slid out from under the covers. "Hi there Bob."

"Hey there, you under the covers," as I took her hand, she pulled me over for a kiss. In no time my hand was under the covers discovering she was in her birthday suit. Now, I was fully dressed with shirt and tie, and her date said he would be back, shortly. Speed was of the essence! First, I took off my shoes, then off came trousers and boxer shorts; with socks still on along with shirt and tie, I hopped in bed with her. Boy! She was good. We passionately, made love!

What does this have to do with Love and War and the intertwining thereof? Absolutely nothing – and everything!

I was fully dressed and having a drink in less than twenty minutes, and just in time, as Jim returned. The Kid finally came out of the adjoining room at my urging because we needed to go. With drinks in hand, we boarded the elevator and returned to our waiting car. Those there were not so happily awaiting our return. We had only been gone half an hour and Ruth was very cool towards me. Our dates had a 10 o'clock curfew and we barely made it back to the William and Mary campus in time. However, we had pushed girls through dorm windows before and gotten by with it every time. I wondered if Ruth suspected I had been up to some kind of shenanigan!

Lest I fool myself into thinking the girl under the covers preferred me to Jim, I found out that Maggie was a nymphomaniac. I had no compunction in making love to another while being disengaged only briefly from my own partner.

Could the war have had anything to do with cheating on my date while out with her the same evening? And how dangerous of Jim, leaving me in the room with her in bed, naked! He possibly, mistakenly, trusted me, and you can't trust a man when along comes a chance to make love, nor when along comes a chance to go to war. The two are interconnected and intertwined.

> *I drink not from the mere joy in wine,*
> *Nor to scoff at faith –*
> *No: only to forget myself for a moment,*
> *That only do I want of intoxication, that alone.*
> *–Omar Khayyam*

We may ask ourselves today as we study history, how much strife and war must we continue to suffer because of some religion. What was Napoleon thinking to come to a conclusion that "love does more harm than good?" It is suggested, prior to his defeat that he had become very weary of war. And Stoessinger wrote, "it is war itself which cures war." Christian love does an awful lot of good helping our fellow man, as do other faiths, but how truthful is it that "love does more harm than good," the love of some religion?

Is it love of power of which he speaks, or possibly the love of gold and silver, or fine jewelry, or some other commodity? Could it be love between two human beings causing more harm than good, to which he refers? There has been much written in romance novels and otherwise about triangle love relationships as the cause for murder. It is just possible that he is simply referring to man's love for war, which does more harm than good. We have all kinds of love and the more powerful is the love of war!

Yes 'n' and how many times must the cannon balls fly before they're forever banned?
The answer my friend is blowin' in the wind.

The Worldly Hope men set their Hearts upon
Turns Ashes — or it prospers; and anon,
Like Snow upon the Desert's dusty Face
Lighting a little Hour or two — is gone.

—Omar Khayyam

AFTERWORD

We have been at war in Afghanistan for over eight years, and I say it's time we let the Afghans settle their own civil war. Our hope of ever catching Osama bin Laden, the needle in the haystack, is long past. Let those who wish to war, continue to war. Remember! It is war which cures war. I wish for our troops to experience some of that highly prized time, called peace.

We have too many military generals! Their job is war and the answer to one of the reasons we go so often. Is there any chance we could have a few civilian generals whose only job is the search for peace?

"World War II was, quite simply, the most deadly, and destructive war in human history." And we call it the "Good War." Why do we call something so devastating, and really horrible, good? I suppose there are valid explanations for naming it such, but it seems incredulous, and lacking in vocabulary, that we can't come up with a better description.

It was originally estimated that around 20 million Russians died in WW II but more recent research puts the number at 26.5 million because Stalin underestimated intentionally, the number of military and civilian casualties. Almost all those Russian POWs died in German camps, mostly from starvation, the number is estimated at 3.3 million. Russian POWs surviving captivity, in most instances failed to survive the wrath of their own liberating army. The USSR was not a signatory to the Geneva Convention, nor was Japan. As might be expected, not many German POWs survived their captivity in Russian camps.

More than sixty million people died in WW II (the good war) and that kind of estimate lends credence to the argument that wars are necessary to keep growth of the world population in check. Otherwise, there would not be enough food, and hell on earth would become more of a calamity! The Chinese loss is put at 4 million and the Japanese 1.9 million. The USSR by far, was the heaviest loser, of all World War II participants. Americans had about 400,000 killed and our British ally lost a half million. A more definitive number cannot be determined because all sources give a different number.

The Iraq and Afghanistan wars have already cost us over a trillion dollars and continue to grow. However, it is not only the ongoing wars taking us towards insolvency, but also the cost of past wars. The health care of veterans from all recent wars but mainly WW II is a major drain on our resources. There are the many wounded, and some wounded requiring specialty care, and the Veterans Administration is strapped for funds. It pays out billions in compensation claims because there is a growing stream of needy veterans. This is the other part of our broken health care system, not addressed in the halls of Congress. It would not be a vote getter for a congressman to question how we are going to pay for veterans' care. This is another one of the more difficult issues facing our Republic!

"Power tends to corrupt, and absolute power corrupts absolutely." This is a quote from 1887, by John Dalberg-Acton with which we are so familiar. Have we given too much power to one man (the President) when it comes to going to war? I fear we have, even with other checks and balances.

We love war and we must thwart that kind of loving if we want to survive. That's a tall order but if we are to endure we must untangle our intertwining of love and war. It is war and the continuation of war, which is the history of the fall of empires. We are the one remaining super power, and the best hope on earth. The great dilemma is our being long on war and short on love.

Oh come with ole Khayyam and leave the Wise to talk,
One thing is certain, that Life flies,
One thing is certain, and the Rest is Lies,
The flower that once has blown for ever dies.
—Omar Khayyam